THE
LIVING
WOODLAND

THE
LIVING
WOODLAND

A
Journey through
the Seasons

DAVID BOAG

BLANDFORD

A BLANDFORD BOOK

First published in the UK 1992
by Blandford
(a Cassell imprint)
Villiers House
41/47 Strand
LONDON
WC2N 5JE

Distributed in the United States
by Sterling Publishing Co., Inc.
387 Park Avenue South, New York, NY 10016-8810

Distributed in Australia
by Capricorn Link (Australia) Pty Ltd
P.O. Box 665, Lane Cove, NSW 2066

British Library Cataloguing-in-Publication Data.

A catalogue record for this book is available from the
British Library.

ISBN 0-7137-2294-0

Typeset by MS Filmsetting Limited, Frome, Somerset

Printed and bound in Hong Kong
by Dah Hua Printing Co. Ltd.

CONTENTS

PREFACE

TO MOST OF US the wood is a place of perpetual interest, with its great diversity of wildlife and views to please the eye. In this book I hope I have captured just a few of the things that I found of special interest, after spending many hours wandering through a variety of woods. However, the wood is not just a place of interesting sights; it is also a mixture of evocative sounds and delightful smells. What a pity it is that within the pages of a book one cannot capture the excited laughing call of a green woodpecker or the garlic scent of ramsons.

To add to the fascination, each wood has its own sense of history. When the acorn that was the beginning of what is now a mighty oak tree first sprouted through the soil, life in Britain was very different: no sound of machinery disturbed the peace of the wood then. And many trees have outlived generations of kings and queens.

We think of the wood as a wild, or natural, environment; indeed, we even refer to the 'wild wood'. It is true to say, however, that almost every area of woodland in the country has been influenced by the hand of man. At one time much of Britain was wooded, but eventually most was cleared to permit cultivation to take place. Timber was always highly valued and a whole variety of craftsmen and foresters grew up relying on the woodland for their livelihoods.

Standing with your back against the solid, towering pillar of a tree trunk, you cannot help being aware of the continuity of life that exists within the wood. I have presented to you, in the pages of this book, a series of individual photographs, but in reality each of them is joined — an ebb and flow of life, each species affecting another. Trees produce the leaves upon which insects have come to rely; birds flit through the canopy in search of insects and then carry them to the ground to feed their young in a nest hidden in the trunk of a rotting tree; and so it goes on.

We have a tendency to divide nature up into convenient slots — most obviously with regard to the seasons — but I have often claimed that for anyone with any enthusiasm for the subject there are 365 seasons to the year, and something new to be found and enjoyed every day! However, for this book I have conformed to conventions, and I hope you will enjoy sharing with me the seasons of the wood as much as I enjoyed creating the book.

SPRING

ACCORDING TO THE CALENDAR the first day of spring arrives on a precise date, but the woodland is in no way influenced by the precise timing of man. It arrives when it will and how it will, affected mainly by the ground temperature and day length. In some years it seems as if it will never arrive, but then suddenly buds are bursting on the trees, plants are flowering and birds are claiming their territorial rights with song. In other years the same process seems to take place in slow motion. However, of one thing we can be certain. Spring will inevitably arrive, bringing new life into the woods.

The gradual increase in temperature and the imperceptible lengthening of the days trigger a great deal of activity in the woods. The first most noticeable change is within the ground cover. Forcing their way through the leaf litter, a host of plants emerge to greet the new season. In some woods a great diversity of plants appears, while in others a single species forms a complete blanket. It is not unusual to discover a green carpet of dog's mercury or a white sheet of ramsons, and all of us enjoy the sight of a haze of bluebells.

Now that the plants have brought spring into the wood, hibernating insects are able to emerge to feed on them. Eggs of insects that have remained dormant throughout the winter now hatch. As a result, the freshly burst buds on the trees are under constant attack from the multitude of insects that are wanting to feed on the soft new growth.

The dramatic increase in the insect population encourages birds to begin their breeding cycle and the resident birds are soon joined by migrants that have travelled many hundreds of miles to nest in our woodlands. Within the riot of bird-song it is easy to overlook the effect of spring on certain species of birds. Redwings and fieldfares, for example, leave our woods to breed in environments more suited to their needs.

As each creature and plant take advantage of spring in their own ways, they cannot help affecting the other life that surrounds them. Whether it is a caterpillar eating a leaf, a woodpecker drilling a hole into a tree or the canopy of leaves blocking out light for the ground plants, everything has its part to play, striving to survive and multiply, each needing the other.

Although snowdrops produce their delicate flowers in the depths of winter, to many of us the sight of these little flowers contains the welcome promise of approaching spring. It is surely one of nature's miracles that such a frail-looking bloom should be produced during the most harsh time of the year.

Primroses are one of the most familiar flowers to be found in the woodland during the early spring months. It would seem that the name of the primrose derives from *Prima rosa* or 'first rose'.

Feeding upon the sweet nectar produced by the primrose, a brimstone butterfly is well camouflaged. This butterfly would have over-wintered as an adult insect, hibernating deep in the shelter of an ivy-covered tree, and is one of the earliest butterflies to appear in the spring. The male is easy to identify: any large yellow butterfly in flight at this time of year is certain to be a male brimstone. The females are less distinctive as they appear white and closer inspection is needed to identify them. The underwings of the brimstone have a greenish tinge and prominent veins create a leaf-like effect.

Violets are also important to some butterflies because their leaves provide the food for the caterpillars of several species of fritillary. During the spring violets mix with primroses, decorating the woodland floor with their distinctive colours.

Perhaps it is because so many daffodils are found in cultivated gardens that one assumes daffodils found in the woods must have been planted by humans. However, the wild daffodil is a true native bulb that can be found in many areas of England and Wales. The plants are generally smaller than the cultivated varieties, but their bobbing yellow heads are still a sure sign that spring has arrived.

In the topmost twigs high above the woodland floor, a rook has built its nest early in the year. A rookery may contain dozens of nests, each pair intent on raising its own youngsters to continue the species. Although these birds use the trees of the woodland to nest, they search the surrounding farmland for insects and grubs with which to feed their young.

It is understandable that the grey heron is generally thought of as a waterside bird. However, even the heron spends a great deal of time in the high branches of the wood. Early in the year it will return to its traditional tree-top site and reinforce last year's nests with a collection of new twigs. Three to five greenish-blue eggs are laid as early as February or March. During the incubation period and while feeding the young, many herons will perch on nearby branches to rest from their efforts. It is not until May or June that they desert the wood and their raucous noise no longer echoes though the trees.

Like white stars, the flowers of the wood anemone cover the ground beneath the trees. Slender stems hold delicate flowers above the carpet of leaves. They are popular with bees and certain flies that arrive in search of pollen. On dull days the flowers remain closed and droop downwards, awaiting a sunny spell during which, once again, they can attract insects.

Flowering from February until May, the lesser celandine finds every possible opportunity to become well established. Banks, hedgerows, damp bare ground and especially woods are very quickly colonized by this bright golden-yellow flower.

Even the largest tree in the wood began life as a tiny seedling that pushed its way up through the leaf litter. Countless thousands of beech masts sprout from the ground, lifting their cotyledons to the sunlight. Each seedling has the potential for a life spanning some 200 years, but few will survive even the first summer.

Usually the wood pigeon feeds on the ground, collecting seeds, berries and nuts. However, as the buds begin to open on the trees they change their habits and start to feed on the soft fresh growth. A rather large and heavily built bird, it tends to look clumsy as it attempts to pluck a bud from a slender, bouncy twig. In the woods this pigeon is a very shy and wary bird, but where it has become established in town gardens it can be remarkably tame.

The silver birch is one of the first trees to become naturally established in the formation of new woodland. Its winged seeds are tiny and spread in profusion, germinating rapidly to invade new areas. The flowers of birch trees take the form of catkins and although the male catkins first develop during the autumn, they remain small and tightly packed until the spring. During April or May they lengthen into the familiar long, dangling shapes, and as the scales separate, the pollen is released into the breeze.

Buds burst open on the oak tree and produce a hint of colour that is reminiscent of autumn. Rapidly the leaves appear, soft, tender and vulnerable to the attack of insects. At the same time as the new leaves arrive, the oak tree's flowers develop and during May they add to the new growth.

Sharp, hard spines contrast with the soft and gentle beauty of the blackthorn blossom and the decorative effect is added to by lichen. This prickly shrub, or small tree, is commonly found in woods and hedgerows, but because it requires plenty of light it favours clearings or wood-edge locations. One feature of the blackthorn is that the blossom appears before the leaves are produced and this separates it from the hawthorn, with which it is sometimes confused. During autumn, when the fruits are present, it is more often referred to as sloe.

Having hibernated all winter, the comma butterfly becomes active again towards the end of March. It settles frequently on rough tree bark, expanding its wings as it basks in the spring sunshine.

Probably the most common bird to be found in the countryside is the chaffinch. A pair will select a secret site in a bramble bush in which the female constructs her delicate nest while the male sings on a nearby perch. The most usual number of eggs is five and they are incubated for about twelve days before they hatch.

Overleaf
Dog's mercury covering the woodland floor during March.

The tangled mass of twisting stems gives a jungle effect to the woodland. Climbing stems of the traveller's joy may reach up into the canopy level of the wood. The plant is not strong enough to support its own weight, so it can grow only when supported by the trees. During autumn the ripe seeds have long silver-grey curly awns and these are what gives the plant its other popular name, old man's beard.

No matter what the season, starlings enjoy bathing in a puddle of fresh water. Once the splashing is complete, they select a favourite drying and preening post or rest amongst the white blossom of a hawthorn bush. The iridescence of their plumage is lost when the birds are sodden with water, but their quarrelsome and noisy characters are not dampened. Feeding in a more open environment, starlings return to the woods to nest and roost.

Despite its small size the weasel is an extremely successful predator. Its body is lithe and muscular, and it is very agile, fast-moving and strong for its size. Feeding mainly on small rodents, including mice and voles, it will also take birds and their eggs, and even frogs. A good illustration of its power as a predator is that the weasel can even kill a rabbit that is much heavier than itself.

Hiding in the cover of a bush, a song thrush fledgeling takes a fearful look at the world. A few moments ago it left the comparative security of the nest and now it calls plaintively for the attention of its parents. The adults will attend to its needs for a few days before continuing the season with a second brood.

Soft and downy, beech leaves look fresh and delicate in the early-morning sunshine.

Best known of all the woodland plants must surely be bluebells. Covering the ground beneath the trees, the purple-blue haze of flowers is a familar sight throughout May. Growing in amongst the bluebells, other plants also thrive and greater stitchwort produces pure-white, star-like flowers that mingle with the bells. Because the stems of the stitchwort are weak and spindly, they need to be supported by other plants. Red campion has a strong stem that holds its flowers high above the sea of bluebells and may continue flowering well into the summer.

Delightfully acrobatic and often approachable, the long-tailed tit is one of nature's entertainers. It is a beautiful little bird, whose length is doubled by its very long tail. The nest of the long-tailed tit is one of the most remarkable to be found in the woods. Hidden in bramble, hawthorn or gorse, the oval nest is constructed mainly of moss and held together with cobwebs and hair. Once the general shape is completed, including the side entrance, the exterior is decorated with lichen and the interior lined with feathers. The eight to twelve youngsters that are raised in the nest cause it to bulge and, during the last few days, one chick always seems to be calling from the entrance.

In a sunny clearing amongst the trees a red admiral butterfly rests for a few moments on a bluebell. Each year the over-wintering population is added to by large numbers arriving from the Continent. The females seek out nettle beds, where they will lay their eggs and the little caterpillars can feed on the leaves.

Beautiful flower spikes of the early purple orchid can often be found in the woods from April through to June. As its name implies, the early purple is the first of the woodland orchids to flower and, as a result of its liking for shady places, it is often found in the company of bluebells.

Constant clamouring by the young chicks ensures that parent mistle thrushes are kept busy throughout the spring. The fledging of a brood is the end of a long process that began during the winter. The thrushes had first to find and maintain a territory, declaring its ownership with superb song. A suitable site was then approved by the pair before the task of nest-building could begin. Egg-laying and incubation took precedence for a few weeks until the chicks at last hatched. At least two more weeks were needed as they attempted to fulfil the demands of the chicks. After all this effort, it is probable that they will attempt a second brood.

The massive smooth grey trunk of a beech tree holds layer after layer of leaves to the sunlight. The floor of the wood is quickly cast into deep shadow as the soft, limp leaves unfold from the buds. During April they are pale green and fringed with silvery hairs that give them a translucent quality, but this will last only a few days before they mature.

Although the sycamore is not a native tree of the British Isles, it has been cultivated both for its timber and as a shelter tree for many years. The fruits develop during the spring but remain on the tree until the autumn. During the summer they will change colour, often to a bright russet, before falling. Their broad wings make the seeds spiral down, catching the breeze to aid distribution.

Ash leaves develop from out of very tight, small, black buds. They are later than most other trees of the woodland and quite often it is well into May before the tree is fully in leaf.

Purple moor-grass is usually associated with the acid, damp soil of heathland. It is a perennial that always grows in tussocks and here it has established itself in a wood. During the spring the evenly spaced tufts look as if they are wearing green wigs, but later in the year the prolific growth covers the woodland floor.

Overleaf
The garlic scent of ramsons fills the air as one approaches a wood early in the year.

During May silvery-blue butterflies can be found flitting along woodland paths and open glades. They are most likely to be holly blue butterflies, which are the only blues not associated with grassland or heath. The caterpillars feed both on the flowers and berries of holly and also on a variety of other woodland shrubs. A second and larger brood of holly blues is in flight during midsummer.

Hidden within the undergrowth the herb robert plant manages to lift its flower head clear of the vegetation. This fragile little flower is an annual plant that can commonly be found in the woods.

The appropriately named orange tip butterfly is conspicuous in flight, but only the males have the bright-orange colour on the tips of their forewings. The underwings of both the sexes appear to be mottled white and green, but the butterfly is in fact unable to produce a green pigment on its wings and to create the effect, black and yellow scales are mixed together. This means that when settled, the buttefly is provided with a most effective camouflage.

A casual observer watching a great spotted woodpecker feeding is left with the impression that the bird is just tapping the bark. In fact it is hitting the tree with tremendous force, sending chips of bark and wood flying in all directions, in its search for hidden food. When the serious task of nest construction begins, the pair will select partly rotting timber and drill a hole deep into the tree. Here the eggs are laid in the secrecy and security of the nest cavity.

Back-lit by the early morning sun, water avens have found a damp patch of ground in which to flower. It is by no means exclusively a woodland plant, but given the opportunity it thrives in the shade that the trees provide.

Scampering mouse-like up a trunk, a tree creeper disappears into a crevice behind the broken bark of an old tree. This is the most common location for tree creepers to hide their nests. Their slender bills are ideally suited to extracting insects as they methodically work their way from tree to tree, searching every nook and cranny.

SUMMER

AT WHAT STAGE spring slips into summer is hard to determine. Perhaps it is when most plants have emerged from the soil, or when the trees are in full leaf. Indeed, many plants of the woodland floor have completed flowering and are setting their seeds in preparation for next year. Walking through the woods in midsummer, it is clear why the flowers must appear so early in the year, because the floor is now in heavy shadow. Leaves on the trees are peppered with holes and ragged from the attention of so many caterpillars. Most song birds now have young that are feeding on the insects and many pairs of birds will be attempting a second brood.

Although largely unseen, summer is a time when mammals are particularly active. The roe deer has her fawn hidden in dense vegetation, and fox cubs that were content to rest underground for much of the day now begin to explore. It is at dusk that the mammals really begin to stir. Perhaps our immediate thoughts are of badgers, hedgehogs or bats, but the woodland floor is also alive with mice, voles and shrews, scurrying busily amongst the leaf litter.

If mammals provide excitement by night, then butterflies provide beauty during the summer's day. Every sunny glade within the wood is brightened by these flitting insects. They move from thistle head to bramble flower, feeding on the nectar, pollinating the plants as they go. As a result the plants produce a harvest of seeds and fruits, and these in turn are eaten by birds or small mammals.

On a hot summer's day, even though the air may be still, the temperature within the wood is always a few degrees cooler. The quietness and peace are somehow exaggerated by the constant buzz of hover flies or the tapping sound of a nuthatch as it chips at the bark of a tree in search of a tasty morsel.

By the end of summer even the larger birds will have fledged their young and most young mammals are becoming independent. Gradually the length of day decreases and the nights become cooler as the summer prepares to merge into autumn.

As the female green woodpecker arrives at the nest, the male wriggles out of the hole to allow her to enter. He will spend an hour or so feeding before he returns to relieve the female of incubating duties. The eggs are hidden deep within the nest and will take between fifteen and sixteen days to hatch. As the young grow, they will take turns at the entrance hole to wait for the incoming parents to feed them, but they remain in the nest for about four weeks.

One of Britain's largest butterflies, the silver-washed fritillary, feeds from a bramble flower. In some woods these beautiful butterflies are quite common and can easily be found in woodland rides from June to August.

Another regular visitor of bramble flowers is the painted lady butterfly. In some seasons huge numbers of these beautiful butterflies arrive from southern Europe and they can be found in every wood, hedge and field. In other years, however, comparatively few are to be found feeding on the nectar-laden flowers.

The small copper butterfly is first to be seen on the wing during May. However, this species is continuously brooded and so it can be found in flight during any summer month, and some late specimens may even be observed as far into the year as October. This splendid little butterfly has the habit of feeding or basking in the sun with its wings half open. The food plant of the caterpillar stage is dock or sorrel and so the small copper is not limited to woodland.

It would seem that fox cubs become bored and restless underground and cannot resist investigating the surrounding woods. When they first come out the vixen is in attendance and they keep close to the earth. As they grow, they become even more inquisitive and, while the adults are away hunting, they wander further from the earth in search of beetles and other delicacies.

Young starlings seem to be noisy and quarrelsome even at the earliest stages. Unlike most other young birds, once they leave the nest they do not remain hidden but leap into life with confidence and great enthusiasm. Perhaps this is because they take a comparatively long time to fledge (three weeks) and are well developed.

A robin fledgeling leaves the nest after less than two weeks of life. Rather than face the world, with all of its dangers, the chicks keep well hidden in heavy cover. It is here that the parents return to feed them, but as the adults' visits diminish, so the young birds discover the insects that live on the woodland floor.

Woodland rides and clearings abound with a variety of wild plants. Flat golden-yellow flowers of fleabane brighten a damp patch of ground, while nearby creeping thistles grow tall in a sunny area. The teasel is a biennial and so it is not until its second year that the strange flower head is produced at the top of a prickly stem. In turn these flowers attract a variety of butterflies, and while a peacock feeds on the thistle, a small skipper sips nectar from fleabane.

Overleaf
As spring melts into summer a woodland path is not only a highway for wild animals but also a place where a range of plants can thrive.

Amidst a blaze of purple foxgloves a few white flowers have emerged. It is possible that each flower spike may bear up to eighty thimble-shaped flowers, so bees, which love to visit them, are kept extremely busy. The plant is a biennial and when in flower is probably one of the best-known and most loved of the native British plants.

In contrast to the popularity of the foxglove, one of the least-loved of wild creatures must be the adder. Its bad reputation comes from the fact that it is the only poisonous snake in Britain, but in truth it is a very timid and shy creature. Flicking out its tongue to taste the air, it retreats to safety as soon as it scents danger.

Like a huge dandelion head, the goat's-beard plant has produced its feathery seeds. A close view of the seed head reveals the wonderful abstract patterns of nature. The flowers open early in the morning but close at midday, which gives rise to its other popular name, Jack-go-to-bed-at-noon.

A pair of kestrels selected a huge tree cavity in which to nest. The eggs were laid during May and now the young birds are close to fledging. Two of the more adventurous chicks have moved to the edge of the nest, where they wait patiently in the sunshine for the adults to arrive. The adults will feed them mainly on mice and voles until they have learned to fend for themselves.

The nest of the chiffchaff is skilfully constructed from grass and moss, then lined with hair and feathers. The domed structure is supported just above the ground in a tangle of undergrowth. During nest-building and incubation the male spends much of his time declaring and defending the territory with bursts of song. However, the song is not very impressive, being little more than a repetition of his own name, 'chiffchaff, chiffchaff'.

The common shrew is a most active creature during both day and night. Presumably because of its small size, it is rarely observed as it scurries busily along runs through the woodland undergrowth. Almost every small creature found in the leaf litter is fair game to the shrew and each day it will eat roughly its own body-weight in worms, beetles, spiders, etc.

At dusk badgers emerge from their sets and, having spent a few minutes stretching and scratching, move off into the shadows of the woods. For most of the night they follow well-worn paths that take them to all corners of their territory in search of food. Although badgers are large mammals, much of what they eat is made up of small animals and their diet consists largely of earthworms, grubs and beetles. To supplement this, they sometimes catch young rabbits, feed on carrion and take fruit or even cereals.

The hedgehog is also an animal that emerges at dusk and shuffles about the woodland floor in search of insects, worms and slugs. It is a nocturnal creature that relies entirely on its coat of prickles for protection. When disturbed it never attempts to escape by running away but simply rolls into the characteristic tight ball, where it sits out the onslaught.

Having spent the winter in Africa, pied flycatchers and redstarts arrive to join the resident woodland birds. Despite its name, the pied flycatcher does not often hawk for flies but rather searches the foliage for insects, especially caterpillars. The females of both the pied flycatcher and redstart miss out on the smart and distinctive plumage of the males; they are a plainer brown. The tail of the redstart, which is coloured bright russet, is constantly quivered by the bird and this eye-catching display gives rise to its name. Both of these species nest in holes in trees. A natural nest site would be an old woodpecker hole but they will take readily to nest-boxes when they are provided.

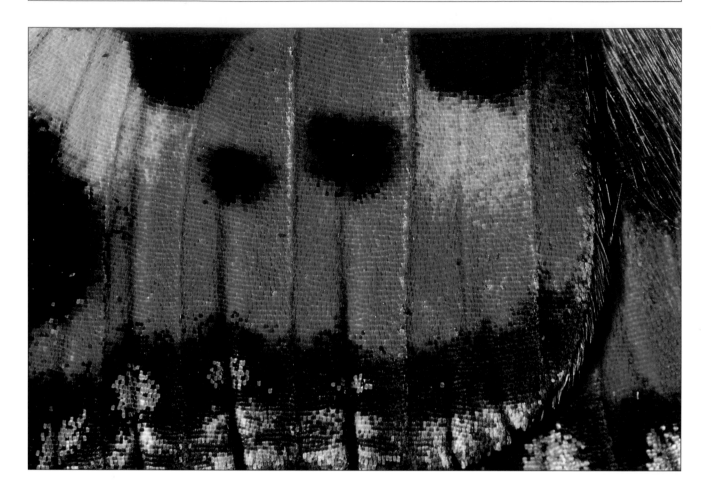

The colourful detail of a butterfly's wing is created by millions of individual scales. Patterns in nature can be quite remarkable and the wing of a small tortoiseshell is no exception.

During the daylight hours a female oak eggar moth hides in a crevice in the rough bark of a tree. Keeping perfectly still, she hopes to escape detection by insect-eating predators. As dusk arrives she will lay her eggs on woodland plants, such as oak, hazel, blackthorn or bramble, to secure the next generation.

Painted lady butterflies visit flower after flower in search of nectar. Once the females are mated, they will leave the flowers to search for thistles on which to lay their eggs. When the eggs hatch, the caterpillars feed on the thistle leaves. A second brood of butterflies emerges in late summer.

Overleaf
Billowing folds of tree-tops stretch into the distance, with thousands of trees creating the woodland that is the home for so much wildlife.

In a tall coniferous tree overlooking the valley a buzzard has chosen to nest. The large structure is built from branches and twigs and is lined with moss and leaves. From time to time throughout the season, fresh greenery is added to the nest. The chicks begin life covered in fluffy white down and when the adults feed them it is with great care. The adults bring a constant supply of food to the nest and as the chicks rapidly grow so the brown plumage appears from beneath the down. Although they may tear a few pieces off, the young birds rapidly learn to help themselves. The main items of prey are rabbits but many small mammals are taken, along with carrion, insects and even earthworms. After six or seven weeks the young buzzards are then fully feathered and leave the nest, eventually joining their parents in their mastery of the air.

There are approaching 300 different species of crane-flies in Britain, ranging in size from the largest, with a wing-span equal to that of a large butterfly, to gnat-like flies. The most commonly recognized we refer to as daddy-long-legs and the larval stage as leather-jackets. These live within the soil, eating roots, and often damage crops.

Slow-worms can often be found basking on a south-facing bank, absorbing the warmth of the sun to gain enough energy to go in search of prey. Unlike some other reptiles, slow-worms do not lay eggs but give birth to live young, usually in a secret location under a flat stone or rotten log. This legless lizard survives the rigours of winter by hibernating beneath the ground, out of the reach of frost.

Because of the threat of a nasty sting, hornets are not popular creatures. The deep buzzing sound they make when they fly and their large size add to the impression of danger. However, the hornet is much less prone to using its sting than its cousin the wasp. The hornet colony is an annual affair because mated queens alone are able to survive the winter, by hibernating in a sheltered corner. The rest of the colony die.

Few woods would be complete without a dog rose growing in a patch of sunlight. The delicate pink flowers are an indication of midsummer because the blooms are at their best in June and July. It is a true native shrub of the British Isles and there is a long history of its fruits being made into rose-hip jelly, syrup or even wine.

Tufted vetch is a climbing herb that has a tangle of weak stems. They cling to other plants for support with the aid of tendrils and during the summer, when they are flowering, the pretty blue-purple, pea-like flowers make an attractive display.

Looking a little dishevelled towards the end of a long breeding season, a female blackbird continues her search for food. Hidden somewhere in the undergrowth her second, or possibly third, brood has fledged and the chicks are waiting for her to feed them. At this time of year blackbirds search the ground for a huge variety of creatures, but especially worms, which they hunt mainly by sight. Berries and fruits will also be added to the birds' diet when they ripen on the hedgerow and woodland shrubs.

Nestled into the soft leaves and twisting stems of honeysuckle, a yellowhammer has built its nest. The yellowhammer is in fact a bird of the open farmland, but it has chosen to make use of the cover afforded by the wood to nest. Though the yellowhammer is a seed-eating bird, instinct tells it that it must gather caterpillars and other insect larvae to feed the young chicks.

Teeming hordes of tiny creatures cover the woodland floor, many of them unseen and more often than not ignored. Perhaps this is because of their small size or their unattractive appearance but, as they busy themselves in their world of leaves, they are performing a vital role in the ecology of the woodland. Working mainly at night, woodlice feed on decaying plant matter, breaking down leaves and rotten wood. Wood ants are effective predators and scour the woods from the forest floor to the tree-tops in search of prey. Centipedes are limited to the soil and leaf litter. They are mini-predators and use poison glands to kill their prey. Hunting the air along woodland rides, broad-bodied libellula dragonflies catch other small flying insects.

A pied flycatcher begins foraging for insects early in the day. It rests for a moment, silhouetted as the thin light of dawn filters through the trees.

Viewed from high above the canopy, the trees are miniaturized and look like soft green parsley covering the ground. Countless millions of leaves that grow, that breathe, that need nourishment and that die — a vital part of our world's ecology.

Patterns of light and shade play across twisted arms of ivy, as they reach up towards the canopy.

AUTUMN

THE EVENINGS DRAW IN a little earlier each day and there is a chill to the night air. Wild creatures that live in the woods are well aware that this is a time when food must be stored in preparation for the long nights of winter. Some will store food by hiding nuts and berries in favoured sites, while others will put on reserves of fat. To many creatures this is an extremely strong instinctive act because an inadequate supply will mean certain death.

In their eagerness to continue the species, trees and other wild plants have produced countless thousands of seeds, berries and nuts. Each one has the potential for life, but very few will actually succeed. It is in the nature of the oak tree to use birds, such as the jay, to distribute and plant its acorns; fortunately it is in the nature of the jay to eat acorns and store them in the ground for winter use. It is during the autumn months that we can observe this symbiotic relationship at its best, with the oak tree exploiting and encouraging the jay's habits by producing far too many acorns and the jay responding by planting more than it will ever find again.

As the first frost of autumn bites into the woodland, many insects are sent scurrying for cover deep into the leaf litter or into the cracks and crevices of tree bark. Many of these insects are destined to die, but the species will be continued thanks to eggs that lie dormant throughout the winter. Flitting among the falling leaves, a red admiral butterfly feeds on the flowers of the ivy well into the autumn months. Soon it will also need to find shelter in the heavy cover of the ivy, which will protect the butterfly as it hibernates through the winter.

The most familiar feature of autumn is the golden glow of colour that is produced by the withering leaves. It is extraordinary that such a riot of colour can be the result of death. As each leaf completes its useful life, it breaks down as many of its valuable components as it can, transporting them back to the trunk and roots. Inevitably it releases its grip on the parent tree and slips to the ground, fluttering and spiralling its way down with countless thousands of others. The woodland floor becomes carpeted with spent leaves that will be broken down by bacteria, fungi and insects, which in turn will return the nutrients to the soil.

The last leaf of autumn is ripped from a tree during an icy gale and the season is swept on into winter.

As autumn arrives the woodland responds by producing a harvest of fruits, nuts, berries and seeds. Each plant and tree will attempt to reproduce itself in its own way; the diversity is as great as the variety of flowers. The seed head of the traveller's joy, or old-man's beard, has yet to mature, but when it does the feathery awns will carry the seeds away on a breeze. Berries of bittersweet change in colour from green to scarlet as they ripen. The shiny berries, which look succulent and tasty, are in fact poisonous to man. Rosebay willowherb often covers a large patch of ground, so when the seeds are dispersing the air is filled with cotton-wool-like seeds, floating in the air.

Previous page
The oak tree secures future generations by producing countless fertile acorns. In a single good year a mature oak may produce several thousand acorns, but in its lifetime of 200 or 300 years, it needs to produce only one surviving offspring to continue the species.

Overleaf
Beautiful colours and patterns are produced by leaves dying on the trees. What a strange quirk of nature, that such beauty is created by death.

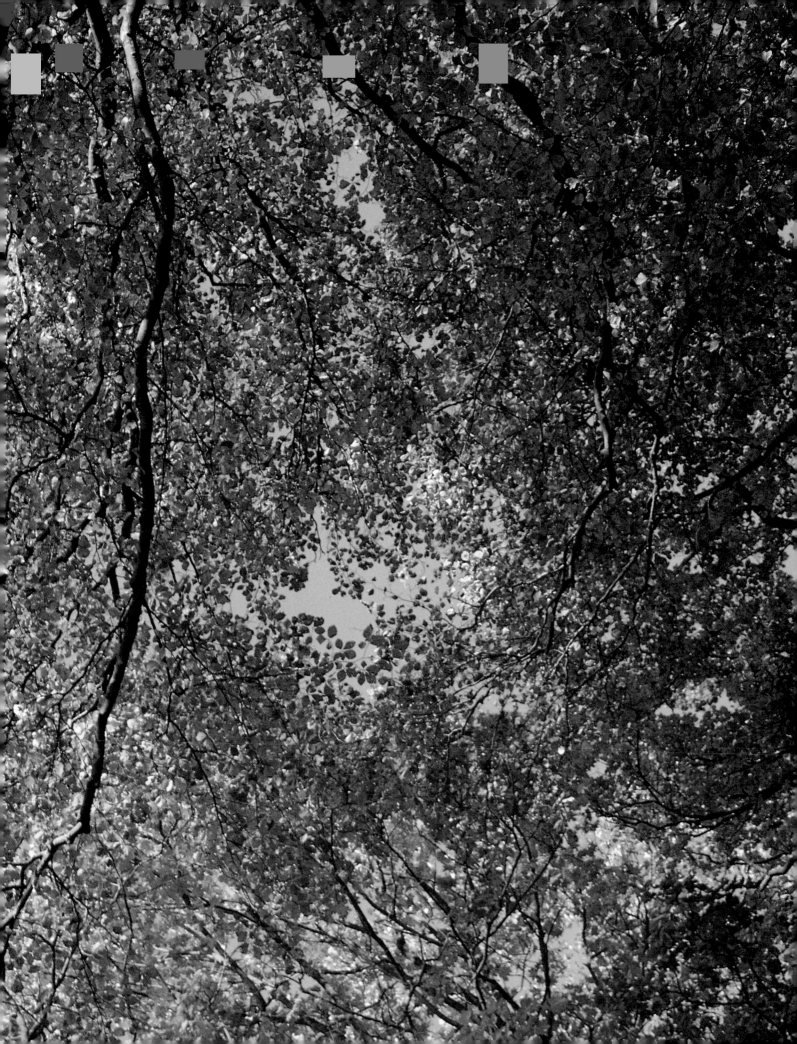

High in the canopy of an oak tree a yellow-necked mouse scampers from twig to twig. It seems to be as at home in the trees as it is in underground runs, and it will even use a tree cavity as a secure place to raise its young. Its large eyes indicate that it is mainly nocturnal. The yellow-necked mouse needs to be alert because it has many predators.

During the day roe deer rest in the security of the woods, hiding in heavy cover. As the sun falls in the sky, they often leave their hiding-places to graze and browse fresh vegetation found along the wood's edge. They remain extremely alert at all times, but now that natural predators no longer exist, they have only man to fear.

The spindle-tree was so named because the wood was close-textured and hard, and so was used for making spindles. The distinctive pink fruits of the spindle-tree are easy to identify because each capsule is divided into four rounded lobes. As the lobes ripen and split, inside a single bright-orange seed is revealed which, although poisonous to man, is a great favourite of blackbirds.

Autumn colours are to be found in the ground cover as well as in the leaf canopy. Bracken that covers the whole of the woodland floor changes to copper-brown as a result of the first frost and remains in this dead state throughout the winter. Overhead huge horse-chestnut leaves create a mosaic of colour and then begin to fall once they have died off.

During the summer nights noctule bats have been feeding on large flying insects. They are one of the largest British bats and often appear comparatively early in the evening. As winter approaches and the nights become colder, the bats are far less active. Having selected a hollow tree in which to shelter, they allow their body temperature to drop and then hibernate for the winter.

The wood mouse is also known by an alternative name, the long-tailed field mouse, and together these names accurately describe the main habitats of this nocturnal creature. Although it is not exclusively a woodland animal, it is a very capable climber and feeds on the bountiful supply of fruits and nuts found in the woods during the autumn and early winter months.

Sunshine, or the lack of it, changes the woodland from a comfortable and welcoming place to an eerie and mysterious one. Early-morning mist clings to spider's webs and spiky leaves of gorse, making every thread glisten with drops of dew. Within an hour the heat of the sun will evaporate away the woodland's temporary disguise.

According to legend, a pot of gold was to be found at the end of a rainbow. As the rainbow arcs down into the trees, it acts as a reminder of the value of our woodland.

By September whitebeam berries have ripened and hang in bright clusters to tempt the birds. Although in only a few weeks they will be stripped bare, it is not the chiffchaff that will remove them. The chiffchaff is an insect-eating bird that will migrate to warmer regions around the Mediterranean, where insects are more easily found.

Neither the chaffinch nor the greenfinch needs to migrate, because their diet consists of mainly fruits, seeds and berries. For them autumn is a time of plenty and an opportunity to put on body-weight in preparation for the colder season. Both of these birds are among the commonest to be found in the woodland, as well as the surrounding farmland and towns.

Overleaf
The woodland trees will stand for many years but the leaves they produce survive only a few months. The fresh green shoots of spring are now tattered and brittle, their work completed, and they drift one by one to the ground.

The hedgehog has been active since the spring but now there is an urgency to its movements. In a few weeks the easily found supplies of food will disappear and the hedgehog will need to find a dry, sheltered nook in which to hibernate during the winter.

Bright-red berries are designed by nature to attract birds to eat them, the indigestible seeds then being passed through and distributed in other areas of woodland. The berries of the stinking iris, or gladdon, are more brightly coloured than the flowers, which indicates the importance of the distribution process. The honeysuckle has used a tree as a support, enabling it to lift its flowers and berries up out of the ground cover.

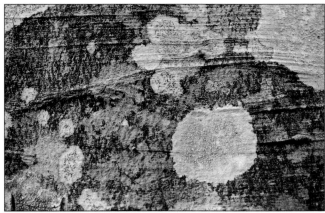

Opposite

On an almost invisible thread, a spider lowers itself from a silver-birch leaf.

Natural patterns within the trees can be discovered at every level. Twisted and gnarled oak roots that grip the soil; lichen-encrusted bark on the trunk of a beech tree; and a flimsy filigree of twigs on silver birch.

It has been claimed that the jay is responsible for the spread of the oak and that without this bird there would be far fewer oak woods. Whether or not this is true, the jay certainly expends much effort collecting and burying acorns during the autumn, with the aim of finding them later in the year. This most attractive bird is strongly attached to the woods, both for its food and also for the cover it provides.

Beneath an ancient oak tree a fallow deer searches the ground for any acorns that may have fallen during the night. The summer coat of this species is beautifully dappled with a random splattering of white spots over the rich reddish-brown coat, but in winter they assume a darker, duller grey-brown appearance. The adult males develop superb antlers, which are broader at the top than at the base.

Autumn is the time when a large number of fungi produce their fruiting bodies. Although unseen, the vegetative stage (known as mycelium) has been active for most of the year, working in the leaf litter or rotting wood. To reproduce they send out fruiting bodies that release spores into the air. Splashes of scarlet amongst the undergrowth highlight the fruiting bodies of the fly agaric, while nearby a fungus known as many-zoned polypore has produced a cluster of velvety brackets.

Hawthorn berries that ripen in September remain on the tree until they are removed by birds during the winter. But it is not only the birds that are interested in these fleshy berries; the haws are an important source of food for wood mice and other small mammals. When they first ripen they are shiny and scarlet, but as the season moves on they become a darker crimson and duller.

Overhead the canopy is changing colour and slowly thinning at the approach of autumn. The strong, dark trunks of horse chestnut and beech reach to the sky, holding the remaining leaves, but even they will soon be swept away by the wind. Although still standing, bracken is brittle and dry and the silver-white trunk of a silver-birch tree is gradually being stripped of its leaves. The woods are silent except for the whisper of the wind as it moves through the branches.

Beech leaves are slow to fall from the trees, and when they eventually do, they are slow to decompose and may limit ground vegetation. The beech masts are ripe by September or October and open to release triangular nuts. The empty shells may remain on the trees throughout the winter and quite often become the hiding places of small invertebrates that are hibernating.

Underground burrows of the bank vole lead into open runways through the undergrowth. From these runways they feed on their vegetable diet of fruits, seeds and fresh green leaves. The bank vole has a long breeding season and young females may become pregnant at only five weeks old. As a result this species is able to increase in numbers very rapidly, but failure of the autumn crop of beech masts or acorns can reduce the population equally rapidly.

Although common, moles are rarely observed due to their underground lifestyle. Their presence is easy to note in the open fields, where molehills indicate recent activity, but in the woods molehills are less often found. However, the mole greatly favours the woodland environment because of its bountiful supply of food. This also means that the mole does not have to dig so much to find food and so fewer molehills are created.

Through the years man has learned to enjoy, ignore or avoid the harvest produced by nature. Some plants, such as the black bryony, are very poisonous and can even cause death, while others may be eaten. Although few people would enjoy eating sloes (blackthorn berries), the fruit has been used for many centuries to make sloe gin or jelly. Rowan or mountain-ash berries we largely ignore, although they were used in the past by the superstitious as protection from evil.

Overleaf
As the last autumn leaves slip from the beeches, winter creeps into the wood and the trees are cloaked with a chill mist.

WINTER

AT THE MENTION OF WINTER one's first thoughts are of frost, snow and ice, but these reflect only a small proportion of the winter days. The variety of weather during winter is as great as at any other time of year, ranging from damp and misty to cold and bright.

Woodland creatures have to be able to cope with these daily changes and they do so, each in their own way. Some avoid winter conditions altogether by migrating; others may leave the woods for a softer life in town gardens; and the most effective way of all is to hibernate. Each of these alternatives has its own problems and dangers, but rather than face the rigours of the woodland in winter, the risk is taken. Animals that do not leave the woods prepare themselves: many insects lay eggs to secure the next generation or pupate in a sheltered corner, while other animals hide away stores of food or put on reserves of body fat. Even when dealing with problems caused by winter, the diversity of nature is astonishing.

Most plant life is at a standstill, but beneath the ground bulbs of spring-time wild flowers are stirring with new life. And this is not the only new life that is stirring underground, because it is during January or February that badger cubs are born in the security of the hidden set.

Although birds such as pied flycatchers and redstarts choose to migrate south, other birds flock into the woods from colder parts of the world. Most noticeable are birds like redwings and fieldfares, which are only found in Britain during winter, but the population of resident birds is increased by continental visitors, and roosts of starlings in some woods can number many thousands during the winter.

Overnight a dull and dreary winter wood may be transformed by patterns of ice or a blanket of snow. But what appeals to our eyes creates new problems for woodland fauna and it is difficult to imagine how small mammals such as voles, mice or shrews are able to continue their bustling lives, even though tell-tale footprints in the snow indicate that they are active.

Imperceptibly the days begin to lengthen and gradually the ground temperature rises, a degree at a time. A few days of sunshine and birds begin to sing, but yet another icy gale sweeps their song away. Eventually, but inevitably, the grip of winter can hold no longer and the cycle of the seasons is completed in the woodland.

Having been foraging on the woodland floor, the grey squirrel prepares to return to the security of the tree-tops. Depending on the season, squirrels feed either on the ground or in the branches overhead, but it is the trees that provide most of their food. Beech masts, acorns and hazelnuts make up a large proportion of the squirrels' diet. Winter is a difficult time for them because food is in short supply and they also suffer badly from damp, cold weather. However, this season was preceded by autumn's abundant food supply and the squirrel survives winter on stored body fat as well as by searching for food that it has hidden earlier in the year.

The mighty beech trees are bare and the woodland floor is littered with leaves. During winter woods can seem strangely silent, almost as if the trees are resting in preparation for another year.

The larva of the December moth will have fed on one of a variety of deciduous trees, typically oak or birch. Then, as its name suggests, the adult moth appears during the winter, flying from October through to December.

It is not uncommon for a beech tree to cling on to a few leaves throughout the winter. For the present a leaf is rimmed with frost, but the sun will shortly melt away this decoration. It is noticeable that young trees are especially loath to lose their leaves.

We have come to regard the red deer as an animal of mountains and open moorland, but in truth its preference is for the more gentle environment of the woods. They have been forced into these less hospitable areas mainly as a result of disturbance by man. Within the woods they feed by browsing on the trees and frequently strip bark from them. Even where red deer are found on mountains and moor throughout the summer, they move down to the shelter of the woods for the winter months.

It is often the case that steep hillsides are heavily wooded. This is mainly due to the fact that they are less suitable for agriculture, the soil being shallow and stony, as well as too steep.

Resident birds, such as great tits, need to be adaptable to survive the difficulties of winter. Although by preference they are insectivorous, insects are difficult to find during the winter. As a result they adapt their diet to include fruit and seeds. Once the breeding season is over, groups of different species of birds gather together and form into large parties. They scour the woodland for food, slowly working their way from one wood to the next.

The robin remains strongly territorial throughout its life, defending its territory against all other birds of the same species. Unlike the tit, it is not constantly moving to new locations; instead, it is able to survive the winter as a result of its intimate knowledge of a small area. It does, however, supplement its diet of insects, worms and spiders with fruit and berries.

An overnight fall of snow changes the familiar into the extraordinary. To assist this transformation a strong wind has plastered the snow to a tree trunk and a bracket fungus also acts as a support.

The coal tit is the smallest of our tits and, being so light, is a wonderful little acrobat. It has a delicate, slender beak that is more suited than the beaks of other members of its family to probing into crevices in search of insects and spiders. This is one bird that is at home amongst conifers as well as deciduous woodland.

The chill of winter has forced a red-legged partridge into the shelter of the woods. The fields are covered with a layer of snow and as a result it has difficulty in finding food. On the edge of the wood the partridge is able to scratch away the snow covering to reveal the seeds on which it feeds.

Overleaf
The air is still and mist hangs heavily in the wood. The call of a pheasant a few yards away seems to exaggerate the silence and enhance the strange atmosphere.

Summer or winter in the yew wood seems to make little difference; it is always dark, silent and forbidding. These huge coniferous trees create a very different type of woodland because within the wood little else is able to live. As a result of the extreme shade throughout the year, nothing can grow on the ground and the floor becomes carpeted with a layer of needle-like leaves. The leaves are slow to decompose and so the carpet can become very thick, and this also prevents plant growth. Apart from birds, which visit the yew trees for their berries, very little animal life is attracted to the wood. Few birds nest there and only a few insects feed on yew. In Britain there are just a handful of substantial yew forests, but they are all extremely ancient, with some trees over 500 years old. Yew trunks are massive and the dark-brown bark is mixed with reddish areas where the outer bark flakes away in strips, and creates natural patterns.

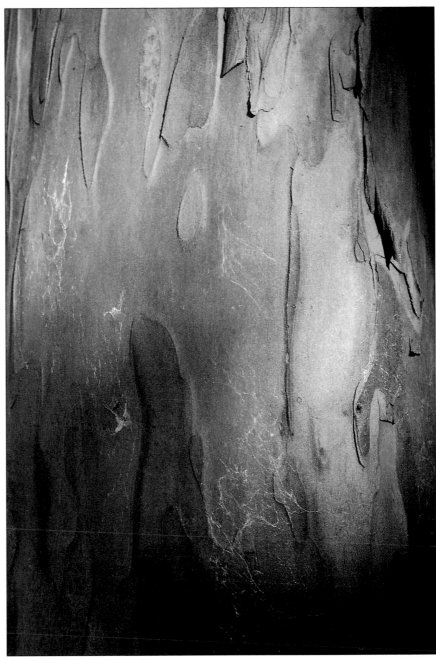

Like many woodland birds, blue tits are willing to leave the woods to visit gardens in search of food. They are popular characters, happy to perform their antics in full view of a quiet human observer. Their ability to hang upside-down on a peanut holder originates in the woodland, where blue tits search for tiny insects that are hidden in the most unlikely places. During winter they are constantly on the move and ringing statistics show that up to 1,000 individuals may pass through one garden in a year.

Freezing fog and a bitterly cold wind have created an ice sculpture on every leaf and twig. Holly berries, a symbol of winter to us, are a welcome meal to the thrush family in these days of extreme cold.

The oak-apple gall is the result of a female gall wasp laying her eggs in the axial bud of an oak tree. The tree responds by producing the growth, and then the larvae hatch and feed inside it. When the adult wasps emerge in July they mate, but the females are flightless and fall to the ground to lay their eggs on the oak roots beneath the soil. The next generation appears sixteen months later and is equally strange, because all members are female, but of two types. They fly up to the oak canopy to lay eggs, one type producing males while the other produces females, and thus the cycle is complete.

Many years ago an acorn sprouted amongst a jumble of huge rocks. As the young tree grew, so the boulders were forced apart, indicating something of the hidden power of nature.

Looking at a healthy tree, it is difficult to imagine that it has a limit to its life. It is true that oak trees may live for several hundred years and that there are yew trees over 500 years old. In contrast, though, the end of most silver-birch trees arrives after only eighty years, and while some beeches may reach 200 years, many will begin to deteriorate after the first hundred. A hollow in the forked branches may collect water, causing the area to rot, resulting in a fallen branch. The tree is now unbalanced and death is imminent.

Rotting wood is an advantage to a nut-hatch because it is able to chip away the softened wood in its constant search for hidden insects. It can climb both up or down a vertical tree trunk with equal ease and investigate the underside of the branches with complete confidence. Nuthatches may draw attention to themselves by a tapping sound which is caused when a bird is opening a nut. It wedges the nut into a convenient crevice and hammers it with its powerful beak until the nut splits, releasing its contents.

A heavy overnight frost has left the woodland painted white with ice crystals. Every brittle twig and leaf is outlined with frost and a slight breeze shakes it down from the trees in little showers, like snow. Between the frozen twigs birds flit from branch to branch, fluffed up against the cold to twice their size.

Using its strong claws and short, stiff tail the green woodpecker makes its way up a vertical tree trunk with a series of jerky hops. It searches the tree for wood-boring insects and, having found a possible spot, reverses to review the area. If the woodpecker sees, or hears, indications of insect activity beneath the bark, it quickly chisels into the wood with its powerful beak. Then, using its extremely long tongue, it winkles the insect out of the exposed tunnel. During the summer it can often be discovered on the ground, where it attacks ants' nests in the same way.

Typically the green woodpecker prefers areas of parkland where there are large gaps between the trees. The edges of mature deciduous woods and woodland rides are equally favoured, providing a similar habitat.

Over the years woodland trees play host to a variety of other plants. Some of these plants grow on but are not fed by the tree; they are known as epiphytes. Others take nutrients out from the tree and are referred to as parasites. At the base of a tall tree, moss clings to the exposed roots as well as the trunk. Halfway up the tree common polypody fern is a good example of a epiphytic plant. In the highest branches mistletoe has become established. Although the mistletoe draws water and inorganic nutrients from its host, it has chlorophyll in its leaves and so carries out photosynthesis to produce most of its own carbohydrates. It is therefore only semi-parastic. From the roots to the twigs, a tree can provide a home for any number of other plants.

Overleaf
Perfect reflections in a woodland pond mirror the winter trees.

Quite remarkable patterns and shapes have been created by hoar-frost. The tiny ice particles have arranged themselves like stars on the needles of a fir tree.

Gently stepping over the snow-covered ground, a roe buck leaves the shelter of the wood. During the winter deer are less able to browse in the trees and shrubs and are forced to leave cover to graze in the fields. A fall of snow makes life even more difficult for the deer, covering the ground and hiding away whatever food there might be. Using their forefeet, the deer scrape away the powdery snow to reveal the grazing that is hidden beneath.

Perhaps the robin can sense the end of winter and the approach of a new breeding season as it sings with renewed vigour. Robins will sing throughout the year to defend their territory, but during the second half of the winter the volume and intensity of their song seem to increase. The robin is notoriously aggressive in its defence of territory, and while to our ears this aggression takes the form of an attractive song of beauty, to other robins it acts as a strong repellent.

As if to hurry spring into existence, snowdrops ignore the harshness of the winter season and bloom in profusion. Irrespective of the calendar, nature's new year begins with the appearance of these delicate little flowers on the floor of the living woodland.

PHOTOGRAPHIC NOTES

WHEREVER I LECTURE, the questions that I am asked relate to photography more often than to any other subject. It is a common misconception that to achieve good results one requires a huge quantity of expensive photographic equipment. I simply use two Nikon camera bodies with four lenses: 28mm wide angle, 50mm standard, 105mm close focus and 300mm telephoto (all Nikkor). I carry these lenses with me all the time, along with a good tripod, a cable release, a low-angle viewfinder, plenty of film (Kodachrome 64) and spare camera batteries. Another bag, containing two flashes, extension tubes, flash cables and other odds and ends, including notebook and pen, usually remains in the car.

Rather than spend too much time on equipment and technical know-how, I prefer to use my enthusiasm, enjoying the life that surrounds me, and to concentrate my efforts on the more creative side of photography.

When considering a subject, I attempt to decide what aspect particularly appeals to me. It could be the colour, the detail, the size, the atmosphere or the character of the subject. This gives me a clearer idea of what it is that I wish to capture, and I can then attempt to exaggerate this feature.

My preference is to use natural light, and if it is possible, I will use the light in two or three different ways, taking several pictures of the same subject. Natural light does not necessarily mean bright sunshine, because some of my favourite photographs were taken in fog. Quite often I am forced to use flash in difficult situations, when the subject is in poor light and moving too rapidly. On these occasions I try to reproduce natural light, and as there is only one sun in the sky, I try to use only one flash and a white card to bounce some light into the heavy-shadow areas.

Some creatures can only be photographed successfully in a studio situation. These would include small mammals and insects. The usual response, from the ill-informed, is that this must be comparatively easy. However, to create and light a small studio set suitable for a mouse, or even a woodlouse, can take a great deal of skill and time.

I cannot explain what it is that enables me to find pictures in a couple of leaves or a piece of bark, but of this I am certain: a superb photograph is never more than a few paces away in the living woodland.

INDEX